Johnny Depp

By United Library

https://campsite.bio/unitedlibrary

Table of Contents

Table of Contents 2

Disclaimer 3

Introduction 4

Johnny Depp..6

Biography...9

Career 12

Privacy policy...26

Legal battle with Amber Heard 30

Filmography 55

Advertising and the arts 65

Other books by United Library 72

Disclaimer

This biography book is a work of nonfiction based on the public life of a famous person. The author has used publicly available information to create this work. While the author has thoroughly researched the subject and attempted to depict it accurately, it is not meant to be an exhaustive study of the subject. The views expressed in this book are those of the author alone and do not necessarily reflect those of any organization associated with the subject. This book should not be taken as an endorsement, legal advice, or any other form of professional advice. This book was written for entertainment purposes only.

Introduction

Johnny Depp takes readers on a captivating exploration of the life and career of one of Hollywood's most enigmatic and versatile actors. From his humble beginnings in small-budget horror films to his iconic portrayal of Captain Jack Sparrow in the blockbuster "Pirates of the Caribbean" franchise, Johnny Depp's journey has been nothing short of extraordinary.

This comprehensive biography delves into Depp's early years, tracing his rise from a teen heartthrob on the television series "21 Jump Street" to his emergence as an acclaimed actor in independent films. With an uncanny ability to transform himself into eccentric and unforgettable characters, Depp collaborated with visionary directors like Tim Burton, delivering mesmerizing performances in films such as "Edward Scissorhands" and "Sleepy Hollow."

The book also explores Depp's remarkable commercial success and critical acclaim in the 2000s, as he navigated diverse roles in films like "Chocolat," "Finding Neverland," and "Public Enemies." Readers will gain insight into Depp's creativity and artistic choices, as well as his foray into producing films and his musical endeavors with the rock supergroup Hollywood Vampires.

Beyond his on-screen achievements, this book delves into the personal life of this enigmatic figure. From his high-profile relationships, including his tumultuous marriage to Amber Heard, to the highly publicized legal battles and defamation cases, the book offers a balanced examination of the man behind the captivating performances.

Featuring stunning photographs and in-depth analysis, this book celebrates Johnny Depp's enduring impact on cinema and provides an intimate portrait of the actor, musician, and cultural icon. It is a must-read for film enthusiasts, fans of Johnny Depp, and anyone fascinated by the captivating world of Hollywood.

Johnny Depp

Johnny Depp, born June 9, 1963 in Owensboro
(Kentucky), is an American actor, director, musician,
guitarist, screenwriter and film producer, receiving
numerous honors during his career, including a Golden
Globe, a Screen Actors Guild Award, a César d'honneur,
three Oscar nominations and two BAFTA nominations.

Depp made his film debut in the horror film *Nightmare on
the Rise* (1984) and appeared in *Platoon* (1986), before
making a name for himself as a teen idol in the TV series
21 Jump Street (1987-1990). In the 1990s, he appeared in
mainly independent films by writer-directors, most often
playing quirky, eccentric characters (*Cry-Baby*, *Gilbert
Grape*, *Benny and Joon*, *Dead Man*, *Donnie Brasco* and *Las
Vegas Parano*) at the same time as beginning his long-
standing collaboration with director Tim Burton, playing
the lead in *Edward Scissorhands* (1990), *Ed Wood* (1994)
and *Sleepy Hollow* (1999).

In the 2000s, Depp rose to fame as Captain Jack Sparrow
in the *Pirates of the Caribbean* film series (2003-2017). He
was nominated for an Academy Award for Best Actor for
the first installment. He also won critical acclaim for *Le
Chocolat* (2000), *Neverland* (2004) and *Public Enemies*
(2009), while continuing his commercial success with Tim

Burton in *Charlie and the Chocolate Factory* (2005), *The Funeral* (2005), *Sweeney Todd* (2007) and *Alice in Wonderland* (2010). This string of successes in the 2000s and early 2010s made him a highly prestigious and recognized actor. In 2012, he was ranked by Guinness World Records as the world's highest-paid actor.

In the 2010s, he began producing films *via* his production company, Infinitum Nihil. He also won acclaim for his performance in *Strictly Criminal* (2015) and formed the rock supergroup Hollywood Vampires with Alice Cooper and Joe Perry, before playing the character of Gellert Grindelwald in *Fantastic Beasts* (2016), and *The Crimes of Grindelwald* (2018). Overall, however, this decade marks a form of decline for the actor, whose films are more and more regularly commercial and sometimes critical failures.

From 1998 to 2012, Depp formed a popular couple with Frenchwoman Vanessa Paradis. The couple had two children: Lily-Rose Melody in 1999 and Jack John Christopher III in 2002. He later married Amber Heard, against whom he subsequently fought a high-profile legal battle. This controversy dented his prestige and kept him away from film sets for two years, before his return in 2023 in the French film *Jeanne du Barry,* directed by Maïwenn, with whom he shares the lead roles.

Biography

Youth

John Christopher Depp II was born on June 9, 1963 in
Owensboro, Kentucky, to waitress Betty Sue Depp (née
Wells) and civil engineer "Jack" John Christopher Depp.
He has one sister: Elisa Christie Depp-Dembrowski (b.
1960), who is very close to him both emotionally and
professionally, working as his assistant and agent for
much of his life, before becoming president of his
production company *Infinitum Nihil*. But he also has a
half-brother, writer Daniel Depp (b. 1953), and a half-
sister, Debbie Depp (b. 1956), with whom they share the
same biological mother"" . He and his family moved
frequently, finally settling in 1970 in Miramar, Florida. His
parents divorced in 1978 when he was 15, and his mother
later married Robert Palmer, whom Depp considers an
"inspiration"' .

His parents gave him a guitar when he was 12. He
dropped out of Miramar High School at 16 in 1979 to
become a rocker, and began playing in a band called *The
Kids*. After modest success in Florida, they moved to Los
Angeles in search of a recording contract, changing their
name to *Six Gun Method*. With no money and no degree,
the musician had to survive in this city-world far from his

rockstar dreams. He would do many odd jobs: mechanic, gas station attendant or telephone pen salesman: "I would play characters on the phone because I was bored. I'd invent names and voices. In the end, it was my first acting class", . At the same time, he reunited with Lori Anne Allison, the sister of his band's bassist and a childhood friend, with whom he married in December 1983. Now a film make-up artist, she knows a number of young actors. They separated in 1985, and Depp began collaborating with the band *Rock City Angels*, where he co-wrote the song *Mary*, which appeared on their first album, *Geffen Records Young Man's Blues*.

Depp is said to be of mainly English descent, with some French, German and Irish ancestors. His surname comes from a French Huguenot immigrant, Pierre Dieppe, who settled in Virginia around 1700. In interviews in 2002 and 2011, Depp asserted his Native American origins: "I guess I have some Native American somewhere on my family tree. My great-grandmother was a bit Native American. She grew up Cherokee or maybe Creek. It makes sense because she's from Kentucky, which is full of Cherokees and Creeks. Depp's claims came under more serious scrutiny when *Indian Country Today* wrote in 2013 that he had never inquired about his heritage and had never been recognized as a member of the Cherokee Nation, as the actor indeed has no documented Native ancestry, leading to criticism from the Native American community, .

Depp's choice to portray *Tonto*, a Native American character, in *The Lone Ranger* (2013) has been criticized, as has his choice to name his rock band *"Tonto's Giant Nuts"*. During the promotion of this film, Depp was officially adopted as an honorary son by activist and politician LaDonna Harris, a member of the Comanche Nation, making him a member of her family but not a member of a tribe. His adopted name is *"Mah Woo May"*, meaning "shape-shifter". Although Comanche Chief Chaiman Coffey declares that he finds the film does not betray his people in the way they are portrayed, and declares Johnny an "Honorary Citizen", criticism from the native community does not abate. A Dior advertisement for *Sauvage* perfume, featuring Depp and Native American symbols, was withdrawn in 2019 after being accused of cultural appropriation.

Career

Debut and revelation (1980s-1990s)

Lori Allison, through her work, introduces her to the young Nicolas Cage, with whom they become friends. Cage advised him to start acting: "I was applying for jobs. I was an unemployed musician and soon to be homeless. My friend Nicolas Cage wanted to introduce me to his agent. He said I could be an actor. Already interested in film, Cage helped him audition for Wes Craven's *A Nightmare on Elm Street.* The inexperienced Johnny says he "ended up acting by accident", . Thanks in part to attracting the attention of Craven's daughter, Depp landed the role of the main character's boyfriend, one of Freddy Krueger's victims. Although he would never look for another job after this entry, Depp declares that he "had no desire to be an actor": "The transition from musician to actor was brutal and confusing. I always felt that at some point I had taken a radical turn without being behind the wheel". He entered drama school and continued to act, earning enough to cover the bills his musical career had not paid. After a starring role in the 1985 comedy *Private Resort*, he was chosen for the lead in the drama Thrashin' (1986) by the film's director, but his producer rescinded the decision. Depp then discovered he was a second-rate actor, appearing in the series *Lady Blue* (1985) and *Death in Troubled Waters* (1986), and appeared in Oliver Stone's drama *Platoon* (1986), but in a minor role as a soldier.

Fox spotted him and cast him in the lead role of *21 Jump Street* (1987-1991), a series that struck a chord with young Americans and was a runaway success, putting Johnny in the spotlight. He apparently accepted the role to work with the actor Frederic Forrest, who inspired him. Despite his success, Depp, who has become an idol for young people, doesn't identify well with the series, believing that it forced him "to play the role of a product": "They force-fed America my face [...] It was a very uncomfortable situation, and I swore to myself that after I left the show, I would do whatever I wanted, however I wanted".

So, of all the film proposals the actor received following the success of *21 Jump Street*, he chose the one that brought him closest to himself and his rock roots, John Waters' *Cry baby* (1990), which relaunched his career with a bang. "It was really the first time I could say: 'I want to go down this road, I want to do this'. But it was Tim Burton who offered him the role of critical acclaim in 1990 with *Edward Scissorhands*. From then on, Tim Burton was his actor of choice and his friend, with whom he also worked on *Ed Wood* (1994), *Sleepy Hollow* (1999), *Charlie and the Chocolate Factory* (2005), the animated film *The Funeral* in 2005, *Sweeney Todd* (2007), *Alice in Wonderland* (2010) and *Dark Shadows* (2012). "We had the same vision of things, the same interpretation, the same humor - it was palpable.

In the 1990s, other collaborations tended to give him the image of an actor shunning big productions, preferring to work with writer-directors with a strong artistic identity. In 1993, he worked with Emir Kusturica, who offered him a role worthy of his talent in *Arizona Dream*, and with Jim Jarmusch in 1995 in *Dead Man*. He collaborated three times with Terry Gilliam: in 1998 in the cult adaptation of the book *Las Vegas Parano* by his friend Hunter S. Thompson, and in the chaotic, unfinished *The Man Who Killed Don Quixote*, which led to the 2001 documentary *Lost in La Mancha* (directed by Keith Fulton). In fact, it was during the preparations for the filming of *Las Vegas Parano* in 1997 that Depp spent four months in the cellar of the house of the pope of gonzo journalism, to immerse himself in the character and forge a sincere friendship between the writer and the actor. After Thompson's suicide in 2005, Depp financed most of the ceremony in his memory, including the scattering of his ashes in the sky by means of a cannon.

After playing a mafia undercover FBI agent opposite Al Pacino in *Donnie Brasco* (1997), he tried his hand at directing a feature film for the first time with *The Brave*, in which he directed Marlon Brando, with whom he had made friends on the set of *Don Juan DeMarco* in 1994. It tells the story of the last days of a young outcast father who agrees to die on camera in exchange for money to lift his family out of poverty. His half-brother, Daniel Depp, helped write the screenplay. The film was presented in competition at the 50e Cannes Film Festival, but following poor American reviews, it was not distributed in American cinemas.

In recognition of his extensive filmography, in 1999 he was awarded an honorary César for his body of work. That same year, his attachment to France enabled him to star in the fantasy film *The Ninth Gate* (*La Neuvième Porte*), shot largely in Paris under the direction of Roman Polanski and starring the latter's wife, Emmanuelle Seigner. Reviews were mixed, however, and the film did not fare well at the U.S. box office. He had better luck with his second European effort, the romance *Le Chocolat*, shot in Burgundy with Juliette Binoche, which attracted more critical acclaim than he did. He would not conclude this French period until 2004, when he appeared alongside Charlotte Gainsbourg in Yvan Attal's comedy-drama *Ils se marièrent et eurent beaucoup d'enfants.*

Commercial success and critical acclaim (2000s)

But just as these roles were undermining his status as a profitable actor, in 2002 he was given the role of Jack

Sparrow in Disney Studios' blockbuster *The Curse of the Black Pearl*. He was given carte blanche to build this complex, elusive character. Released in 2003, the film was a surprise, and a huge critical and commercial success, re-launching Depp's career as a *bankable* actor, bringing him to the attention of young audiences, and even earning him his first Best Actor Oscar nomination. He thus regained his status as a profitable, riot-triggering actor that had driven him away from *21 Jump Street*.

His next film was *Rochester, the Last of the Libertines* (2004), in which he co-starred with John Malkovich. The film tells the story of a famous poet from the 17th[e] century, a notorious debauchee and free-thinker under the reign of King Charles II of England. The film went unnoticed, but not the biopic *Finding Neverland*, in which he played the poet John M. Barrie, and starred opposite Kate Winslet. The film received excellent reviews and earned Depp his second Best Actor Oscar nomination.

That same year, Depp shot the next two installments in the *Pirates of the Caribbean* franchise: *The Secret of the Cursed Chest (*2006) and *To the End of the World* (2007), confirming the success of the first installment. This success was more than profitable for the film's core team: Johnny Depp, Orlando Bloom and Keira Knightley (actors), Gore Verbinski (director), Jerry Bruckheimer (producer) and, of course, the Disney Company. In 2006, he lent his voice to the video game *Kingdom Hearts 2*, where he reprised his role as Jack Sparrow in the Port Royal level, the city in which the *Pirates of the Caribbean* series is set.

In 2007, he reunited with Burton for the lead role in the musical *Sweeney Todd: The Evil Barber of Fleet Street, for which* he won the Golden Globe for Best Actor in a Motion Picture Musical or Comedy, as well as a third Best Actor Oscar nomination. In 2009, he played the role of notorious gangster and bank robber John Dillinger in Michael Mann's *Public Enemies*, alongside Christian Bale and Marion Cotillard. He appeared in *The Imaginarium of Doctor Parnassus* in 2009 (replacing actor Heath Ledger, who died during filming, for a single sequence).

Commercial success and departure from Hollywood (2010s)

In early 2010, he played the Mad Hatter in the Disney Studios blockbuster *Alice in Wonderland*, 7[e] directed by his friend Tim Burton, which grossed a total of $1 billion. That same year, he starred as Franck Tupelo in late 2010 in Florian Henckel von Donnersmarck's *The Tourist*, opposite Angelina Jolie (the American version of the French film *Anthony Zimmer*). *The Tourist was* a commercial success, grossing over $278 million at the box office worldwide, despite very mixed reviews. In 2011, he lends his voice to the main character in the animated film *Rango*, directed by Gore Verbinski, director of the *Pirates of the Caribbean* trilogy. At the same time, he was directed by Rob Marshall for *Pirates of the Caribbean: The Fountain of Youth*, the fourth installment in the saga, this time starring Penélope Cruz.

Finally, he returned to his first love in *Rhum express*, the second film adaptation of a book by gonzo journalist Hunter Thompson, after *Las Vegas Parano*. It was while Depp was staying at Thompson's house that the actor discovered a long, unpublished short story by the author, and learned that it was in fact his very first novel, which had never before been published. After reading it, Depp convinced Thompson to adapt it for the screen. In the meantime, the novel *Rhum express* was finally published and enjoyed great success in the bookshops, but the two friends had difficulty finding real financing for the production of this strange, offbeat film. It was after Hunter S. Thompson's suicide in 2005, Johnny Depp decided to produce a film adaptation of the book himself, and to once again play his late friend on screen as a tribute to him. Thanks to his fortune as one of Hollywood's highest-paid actors, he was able to move far away from Disney America, to Puerto Rico, and finally finance the film.

In 2012, he reprised the lead role in a new Tim Burton film, *Dark Shadows*, starring Eva Green and Michelle Pfeiffer. The actor stars as the vampire Barnabas Collins.

The film is an adaptation of an American TV series of the same name, *Dark Shadows*, broadcast in the late 1960s. The same year he made a cameo in the film adaptation of the series that made him famous, *21 Jump Street*, starring Jonah Hill and Channing Tatum. In 2013, he played the Indian character Tonto in the blockbuster *Lone Ranger, Birth of a Hero*, Disney Studios' third attempt to create a franchise around the actor. On the film's release, Comanche Chief Chaiman Coffey declared that the film did not betray his people in the way they were portrayed; after the film, Johnny Depp was declared an "Honorary Citizen" and christened *Mah-Woo-Meh*, meaning "Chameleon" or "He-who-metamorphoses". However, *Lone Ranger was* a critical failure and a box-office disappointment.

In 2014, Johnny Depp stars as a scientist whose mind has been virtualized by a computer in *Transcendence*, the first film by Wally Pfister (Christopher Nolan's cinematographer). The film was another box-office failure in the U.S., receiving negative reviews overall. After a critical and commercial flop with the comedy *Charlie Mortdecai*, Johnny Depp finally reconnects with critics thanks to his performance as gangster James J. Bulger in the thriller *Strictly Criminal* in 2015, which performs honorably at the box office. That same year, he was inducted as a Disney Legend.

That same year, he returned to the realm of musical comedy with *Into the Woods! Promenons nous dans les bois*, an adaptation of another play by composer Stephen Sondheim, adapted for the screen by Disney Studios. A bold retelling of the Grimm brothers' fairy tales, he lends his features to the role of the Wolf. He completes a prestigious cast that includes Meryl Streep, Emily Blunt, comedian James Corden and Anna Kendrick. The film marks his second collaboration with Rob Marshall. A huge success in its home country, the musical has struggled to find an audience in Europe.

In 2016, he reprised the role of the Mad Hatter in *Alice Through the Looking Glass*. The same year, David Yates, director of the last four *Harry Potter films*, officially announces that Johnny Depp will play the Dark Mage Gellert Grindelwald in *Fantastic Beasts*, the first film in the saga derived from the Harry Potter universe. The actor made a brief appearance in the film, then returned to the role of Grindelwald in the second *Fantastic Beasts* (2018). In 2017, he starred in the fifth and final installment of the *Pirates of the Caribbean* saga, once again taking on the role of Captain Jack Sparrow. During filming, he was reportedly "constantly drunk, alcoholic and unmanageable", according to members of the technical crew, as well as "very often late". His "erratic behavior disrupted the smooth running of the shoot". He went on to star in Kenneth Branagh's *The Crime of the*

Orient Express (2017), Brad Furman's *City of Lies* (2018) and *Les Derniers Jours de Monsieur Brown* (2018).

Media comeback and revival in Europe (2020s)

In November 2020, he lost his case against British tabloid *The Sun*, which had written a controversial article about his marriage to his then-wife: actress Amberd Heard. The two stars became embroiled in a long legal battle that lasted five years. At the time of its publication, the article caused a number of setbacks for Johnny Depp's career. Wishing not to be compromised, the actor declared his withdrawal from *Wizarding World*, having been pressured to do so by his production company at the time Warner Bros - which confirmed the decision in a press release - his role as Gellert Grindelwald in Fantastic Beasts 3 being replaced by that of Mads Mikkelsen"" . Two years later, under pressure from Disney Studios, he officially declared that he would never reprise his role as Jack Sparrow in a *Pirates of the Caribbean* film, due to his legal problems, as well as his past problems with alcoholism, drugs and financial debts (caused by his oniomania)" . The same was true of Warner. A petition was then launched on the Change.org website in 2020 to demand his return as Jack Sparrow, with over 800,000 signatures by early 2023. In August 2021, he was awarded the Prix Donostia for lifetime achievement at the 69[e] festival in San Sebastian, and the 55ᵉ festival in Karlovy Vary made him a special guest to be honored.

On the film front, he was more discreet, appearing in independent productions. He appeared in the war film *Waiting for the Barbarians, playing* the secondary role of a tyrannical colonel alongside British actor Robert Pattinson. Despite being presented at the Venice Film Festival, the film went virtually unnoticed. He then lent his features to the photographer *Minamata* in the biopic dedicated to him.

He then turned to Europe, which seemed to offer him a new lease of life. It was in the guise of French King Louis XV in the historical film *Jeanne du Barry* that he made his comeback as an actor. This blockbuster marks his second foray into French cinema after his brief cameo in *Ils se marièrent et eurent beaucoup d'enfants* (2004), and his first major French-language role. The role was originally intended for Gérard Depardieu, but he quickly turned it down. Unsure at the time, Maïwenn tried to contact the American star to offer him the role, and in 2019, the director and actor met in person in London. After a full day of discussions in French, Johnny Depp accepted the role on the advice of his agent. Especially for the actor, Maïwenn and her team removed dialogue, favoring the actor's charisma and facial expressions over his speaking. Although Johnny Depp has little dialogue in the film, he rehearses his French and tries to erase as much of his accent as possible to match her director's idea of Louis XV. Actors Benjamin Lavernhe, Melvil Poupaud and Pierre Richard complete the supporting cast. Postponed because of the pandemic, then abandoned by Netflix, which was to have been responsible for broadcasting and production, *Jeanne du Barry* underwent a complicated preparation. According to media reports at the time, the chemistry between the two actors seemed to work at the start of filming in July 2022, then deteriorated as the shooting progressed. The tabloids spread rumors about Maïwenn's collaboration with Johnny Depp, which were denied by both actors during the promotion of the film. Johnny Depp confided that he particularly enjoyed working alongside Benjamin Lavernhe, a resident of the Comédie-Française, and befriended him during filming. May 16, 2023: *Jeanne du Barry* opens the 76th Cannes Film Festival and opens in cinemas the same day. The festival's decision to promote the film is questioned by cinema professionals, as in the article "Cannes: actresses denounce a system that supports aggressors" published in the newspaper Libération . The actor's presence was criticized, rekindling tensions surrounding the legal battle between him and his ex-wife, as was the case with Maïwenn, accused by Mediapart president Edwy Plenel of having assaulted him while he was dining in a restaurant in the 12th arrondissement . As for the film itself, even though it was acclaimed at the festival, French critics in general were also very divided. The film quickly became a commercial success in its first weeks of release. It became the second most-viewed Cannes opening film since *Gatsby the Magnificent* (2013), before taking 2nd place at the French box office. The film slips back to 3rd place, but remains stable in its box office. *Jeanne du Barry takes* another step forward in its cinematic exploitation, exporting to the United States and other foreign countries.

At the same time, he announced his return to directing, more than twenty-five years after *The Brave*. He will be directing a feature film about Italian painter Amedeo Modigliani, entitled *Modigliani*. He will direct Italian actor Riccardo Scamarcio in the title role, as well as Frenchman Pierre Niney and American Al Pacino, with whom he will co-produce the film.

He was once rumored to be part of the *Beetlejuice* sequel directed by his friend, director Tim Burton. These rumors have been denied. Unnamed sources point to the fact that the actor has been on the outs with Warner Bros since his legal battle and dismissal from the *Fantastic Beasts* film saga.

Privacy policy

A native English speaker, he speaks and studies French and is said to speak a few words of German.

He was twice voted "Sexiest Man Alive", in 2003 and 2009, by *People* magazine .

The actor is said to suffer from a disorder known as oniomania. In conflict with his wealth manager, the latter revealed that in "twenty years, the star has spent $480 million, an average of $55,000 a day. A ranch in Kentucky, five villas in Beverly Hills ... the actor acquired 14 homes for a total of $75 million ... 200 works of art signed Warhol, Jean-Michel Basquiat, Klimt or Modigliani, 45 luxury automobiles, 70 collector's guitars, thousands of star relics ..." .

Relationships

From 1983 to 1985, Johnny Depp was married to Lori Anne Allison, a film make-up artist born in 1957. In the late 1980s, he was engaged to actresses Jennifer Grey and Sherilyn Fenn, before proposing to Winona Ryder in 1990, with whom he had co-starred in *Edward Scissorhands*. "Madly in love Depp decided to tattoo "*Winona Forever*" on his right arm, which he later changed to "*Wino Forever*" . After a relationship with actress Ellen Barkin in

1994, he had a high-profile relationship with English model Kate Moss from 1994 to 1998. In the same year, he became the companion of French actress and singer Vanessa Paradis, whom he met while filming La Neuvième Porte in France. They have two children: a daughter, Lily-Rose (b. 1999), and a son, Jack (b. 2002). While filming in the Bahamas, he fell in love with *Little Hall's Pond* Caye, which he offered to his family as a favorite vacation spot. On June 19, 2012, they announced their separation after 14 years together and without ever having married, then announced the sale of their property at Plan-de-la-Tour, in the French department of Var . On February 3, 2015, after several years of dating, he married actress Amber Heard, with whom he had shared the screen of *Rhum express* (2011). They divorced on January 13, 2017 .

Addictions and excessive violence

Depp has struggled with alcoholism and drug addiction for much of his life. The actor has spoken several times of the physical and psychological abuse inflicted by his mother when he was a child, while his father was often absent, confiding that she beat him and his siblings. "The verbal abuse, the psychological abuse, was almost worse than the beatings. The beatings were just physical pain. Physical pain, you learn to deal with it; you learn to accept it; you learn to deal with it." Some of the violence inflicted by his mother included "throwing an ashtray, a high-heeled shoe or a telephone, hitting her children over the head", "she had the ability to be as cruel as anyone" . He also confides that he consumed pills initially prescribed to her from the age of 11-12, "to escape the chaotic nature of what we were going through": "I never took drugs, I never had a drink to 'party' as the expression goes, which I hate. It was self-medication, I wanted to anaesthetize myself, I wanted to soothe my brain and feel better. I started at a very early age, around 12, stealing 'nerve pills' from my mother's handbag". Although he admits to having been addicted to opiates for several years, he explains that he "never lost control" . Johnny's sister, Christi Depp-Dembrowski, reiterated these remarks during her hearing at the 2022 trial.

In a 1997 interview, Depp admitted to abusing alcohol during the filming of *What's Eating Gilbert Grape?* (1993). In 2013, he declared that he had stopped drinking, adding that he had pretty much taken all he could get out of it. Regarding his breakup with longtime partner Vanessa Paradis, he says he "certainly didn't rely on drinking to ease the situation or cushion the blow" because "it could have been fatal". According to his ex-wife Amber Heard, Depp "plunged into the depths of paranoia and violence after using drugs and alcohol" during their relationship between 2012 and 2016 . The actor also said that the allegation made by his former collaborators that he had spent $30,000 a month on wine was "insulting" because he had spent "much more" than that amount. During his defamation trial in 2020, Depp admitted to being addicted to alcohol as well as using drugs such as Oxycodone, MDMA and cocaine during his relationship with Heard" .

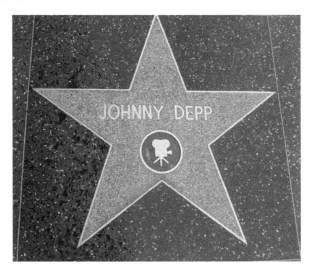

Legal battle with Amber Heard

Johnny Depp and Amber Heard are two American actors who had a relationship between 2012 and 2016. Divorced in 2017, they have since accused each other of domestic violence.

The scandal between the two actors was the subject of much media attention, in the context of the emergence of the MeToo movement after October 2017 in the wake of the Weinstein affair.

The legal battle, illustrated by the two libel suits between 2020 and 2022, revealed many details of their private lives, making public photographs, audio and video recordings, SMS messages and e-mails, but also the testimony of close friends and celebrities.

The first trial - from July 7 to November 2, 2020 in London - pitted Depp against the publishing company of *The Sun* newspaper, which had published his ex-wife's accusations in 2018 and called him a "wife beater". He lost the case, with the British courts ruling that most of the accusations were "substantially true" and "proven". He was not convicted, however.

The second trial - from April 11 to June 1er 2022 in Fairfax - pitted the former spouses directly against each other, and both will be found guilty of defamation. But the verdict is seen as a major victory for Depp, with Heard ordered to pay the actor $10.35 million and the latter $2 million. The two parties had begun proceedings to appeal their conviction before, on December 19, 2022, they retracted their agreement and agreed that Heard would pay Depp one million dollars, thus bringing the court case to a close.

Dating and marriage

Amber Laura Heard (born 1986 in Austin) and John Christopher Depp II (born 1963 in Owensboro) met in 2009 on the set of the film *Rhum Express*, when he was still in a relationship with Vanessa Paradis, and Heard herself was in a relationship with painter and photographer Tasya van Ree. The film was the cinematic adaptation of the book of the same name by Hunter S. Thompson, Johnny Depp's friend and founder of gonzo journalism[ref. needed], who committed suicide in 2005.

The two actors were acting together for the first time, and soon began to bond. At the Santa Barbara Film Festival in 2016, Depp spoke of "love at first sight" . They met again to promote the film, and began dating later, in 2012, when they both ended their previous relationships. They married three years later, on February 3, 2015, in a private ceremony on the actor's Bahamian cay: *Little Hall's Pond*[vii] .

Divorce and first accusations

After a year and a half of marriage, Amber Heard filed for divorce on May 25, 2016 on grounds of domestic violence, and obtained a restraining order against Depp from a Los Angeles court - translated in French as injonction d'éloignement, an order of protection - the actress alleging that Depp had a problem with alcohol and drugs, that he "became a violent monster every time he used", that he had hit her in the face with a cell phone and abused her.

"Throughout our relationship, Johnny Depp verbally and physically abused me," she declares in an affidavit, "I lived in fear that Johnny would return [to our home] unexpectedly to terrorize me, physically and emotionally." Depp denies all of this, claiming that she would use the scandal "to obtain a premature financial solution"[v] .

An agreement was finally reached the same year, Heard removed the restraining order and the divorce was granted on January 13, 2017. They share the assets acquired during their marriage.

Amber Heard publicly pledges to donate her divorce winnings (7 million USD) to the *American Civil Liberties*

Union and the Children's Hospital of Los Angeles (*CHLA*) - a pledge that Johnny Depp will accuse her of not having kept, or of still not having fulfilled, several years later"" .

They state that their relationship "was intensely passionate and sometimes explosive, but always based on love". There was "never any intention of hurting each other physically or morally", and they wished each other "all the best for the future". But the affair had already gone viral, particularly against Johnny Depp, and many are calling for him to be dropped from the cast of the *Fantastic Beasts* and *Pirates of the Caribbean* sequels.

On April 27, 2018, British tabloid *The Sun* (NGN, News International), which relayed Amber Heard's accusations of domestic violence, published an online article written by Dan Wootton, one of the paper's editors, in which he referred to the actor as a "*wife-beater*", accusing him of abusing his ex-wife' . Originally entitled "GONE *POTTY* How *Can* J K Rowling *be 'genuinely happy' casting wife-beater Johnny Depp in the new Fant*astic *Beasts film?*", the article refers to the actor's role as Gellert Grindelwald in the film. On June 1er , Depp decided to sue the *Sun*'s publisher - *News Group Newspapers* (NGN) - and Dan Wootton for defamation. The complaint states that Amber Heard "was not a victim of domestic violence, but the perpetrator"" . The title was changed on June 12, shortly after Depp filed his lawsuit, and was never used in the print version. In their defense, NGN and Dan Wootton allege fourteen incidents of domestic violence by Depp, which were the focus of the London trial.

In December of the same year, Amber Heard wrote an *op-ed* page in the *Washington Post* on the situation of women living with domestic violence. Depp is not mentioned, but the actress refers to him implicitly, writing in part, "I have become a public figure representing domestic violence, and I have felt the full force of our culture's anger toward women who speak out." In March 2019, he publicly declares that he is suing his ex-wife for defamation over this article, alleging that it was a ruse by Amber Heard to curry favor with media opinion. He is seeking $50 million in damages.

In her accusations, Amber Heard details multiple instances of abuse that allegedly occurred during her marriage, presenting photos of supposed bruises on her face after being beaten by her ex-husband. *TMZ* also presents a video filmed by Amber Heard in August 2016, showing the actor drunk at his West Hollywood home, as he violently slams closet doors and kicks furniture. In January 2020, the *Daily Mail* published a series of audio calls in which the actress allegedly confessed to repeatedly beating Johnny Depp: "I can't promise I won't get violent again, I get so angry sometimes I lose control [...] I hit you, but you're fine". In addition to the physical abuse, the actor accuses her of defecating in the marital bed⸍ and cheating on him several times during their marriage, including with James Franco, Elon Musk and Cara Delevingne⸍⸍⸍ .

London trial (2020)

Full name of case: *John Christopher Depp II v (1) News Group Newspapers Ltd, and (2) Dan Wootton.*

Depp's libel suit against *The Sun* newspaper begins on July 7, 2020 . The actor reaffirms that he never hit Amber Heard or any other woman, that she was the violent person in the relationship and further accuses her of cutting his finger with a broken liquor bottle⸍ . The latter reaffirms her accusations of domestic violence, as do the incidents alleged by NGN and Dan Wootton⸍ .

At the trial, Vanessa Paradis testified on the actor's behalf, claiming that he had never been violent with her: "This bears no resemblance to the real Johnny I knew, and from my personal experience over these many years, I can say that he was never violent towards me [...] It's so upsetting because he helped so many people in his personal and professional life, with kindness and generosity [...] He was a kind, caring father [...]. [...] It's so upsetting because he helped so many people in his personal and professional life, with kindness and generosity [...] He was a kind, caring, generous and nonviolent father." In contrast, Ellen Barkin - an actress who had a brief relationship with Johnny Depp in 1994 - described him as a "jealous", "dominant" man, immersed in "a world of violence". She explained that after the first few moments of their relationship, the actor was "drunk all the time" and "verbally violent". Her first sexual encounter with him was said to be one of blurred consent, extracted by the actor administering Quaalude, a recreational drug .

On November 2, the comedian lost the libel suit, with London High Court Judge Andrew Nicolla ruling that 12 of the 14 incidents of violence claimed by Heard and the tabloid were "substantially true", as "the vast majority of the alleged assaults have been proven"[2020] EWHC 2911 (QB) . The court rejected the comedian's defamation claim, but did not formally condemn the domestic violence. However, it did acknowledge that Heard's allegations against him had damaged his career .

Following this verdict, Johnny Depp declared on November 6 that he was withdrawing from *Wizarding World*, having been pressured to do so by his then production company Warner Bros, his role as Gellert Grindelwald in *Fantastic Beasts 3* being replaced by Mads Mikkelsen . Nevertheless, he reaffirmed that the verdict would not change his "fight to set the record straight", and appealed against the verdict. The appeal was rejected on March 25, 2021′ , the judge concluding that it had "no real hope of success".

Fairfax trial (2022)

Full name of case: *John C. Depp, II v. Amber Laura Heard.*

In addition to suing *The Sun*, Johnny Depp is also filing a lawsuit against Amber Heard in early 2019, for her article published by The *Washington Post* in December 2018 in which she speaks out as a victim of domestic violence. This new defamation trial begins on Monday April 11, 2022 in the Fairfax County courthouse in Virginia. The actor, attempting to "clear his name", is seeking $50 million in damages from his ex-wife, alleging among other things that she was the aggressor, that her claims were a fabrication and that as a result, Disney had refused to cast him in future projects′ . Amber Heard, in turn, is claiming $100 million by suing Depp's former lawyer, Adam Waldman, for his numerous statements in a 2020 *Daily Mail* article′ , alleging that they were false and defamatory, that her ex-partner had inflicted "constant physical and sexual violence" on her, but also that he had coordinated a harassment campaign via social networks and online petitions with the aim of getting her fired from *Aquaman* and L'Oréal, of which she is one of the ambassadors″ . Numerous witnesses were called to testify about the relationship between the two actors, including Johnny's older sister Christi Dembrowski, the couple's doctor and bodyguard, as well as public figures such as Paul Bettany, Ellen Barkin and Kate Moss" . James Franco and Elon Musk were also called to testify on Amber Heard's behalf, but the actress's exes have both publicly renounced their participation in the trial' .

After six weeks of closing arguments, the seven jurors retired on Friday May 27 for deliberations. On Wednesday June 1er , they found the actors both guilty of defamation. Amber Heard was awarded **$10** million in compensatory damages and $350,000 in punitive damages. Johnny Depp was awarded $2 million in compensatory damages for comments made by his lawyer Adam Waldman. Depp and Heard will later appeal their respective verdicts, before withdrawing their claim when both parties agree to end their legal battle. Depp's lawyers declared on December 19 that he would finally receive $1 million in damages from Heard, as both parties did not follow the trial verdict that condemned both actors' .

Allegations against Amber Heard

"I'm sorry I didn't slap you properly [...] I didn't hit you. I fucking hit you! [...] I don't know what my hand movement was. But you're okay. I didn't hurt you. What am I supposed to do? I'm not going to sit here and complain like you [...] You're such a baby, grow up Johnny."

"Tell the world. Tell them: I, Johnny, man, am also a victim of domestic violence. And we'll see how many people will believe you and be on your side!"„

- Audio recordings made public in 2020 by the Daily Mail and played by Depp's lawyers in court, where Amber is heard talking to Johnny about his violent excesses.

During Johnny Depp's defense, many close friends and family were called to testify on his behalf„„ . The case of the severed finger from a bottle of vodka„„ and the story of human excrement on the marital bed„ received a great deal of attention. On April 26, psychologist Shannon Curry stated that the actress was suffering from psychological problems, including personality disorder„ .

According to the *Daily Mail*, Heard is also accused of calling the paparazzi when she appeared at the Los Angeles courthouse in May 2016, revealing her "fake bruises" on her face, and also of cutting out part - where she is allegedly laughing - of the video she sent to the *TMZ* media in 2016, in which her drunk ex-husband is seen violently punching furniture„„ .

On May 25, Kate Moss - Depp's spouse between 1994 and 1998 - testified by videoconference to deny the rumors expressed several times by Heard, claiming that the actor had pushed the English model down a staircase during a stay at the Goldeneye Resort in Jamaica. "Johnny left the room before me. There had been a thunderstorm and I slipped on the steps as I left the room. I hurt my back. I screamed. He came running back to help me, carried me to my room and gave me medical attention [...] He never pushed me, kicked me or pushed me down a single staircase"‴ . She repeated her comments on July 24 on BBC Radio 4's *Desert Island Discs*: "I know the truth about Johnny. I know he never pushed me down the stairs. I had to tell that truth".

"When the allegations were made, when they went around the world, telling people I was a menacing drunk on cocaine, beating up women, suddenly, in your fifties, you're done. You're finished. Whatever the outcome of this trial, the second these accusations were made against me, and metastasized into media fodder, I lost. I lost, and I'll carry this for the rest of my life [...].

There's no need for violence. Why would you hit someone to get them to agree with you? [...]

My children refused to be around her, because they were much smarter than I was. They didn't like the way she treated me [...] I could hardly ever go and see my children, spend time with them, because she had to have me with her all the time for her own needs [...]

Mrs. Heard, in her frustration and rage, would strike [...] It might start with a slap, a shove. She threw a TV remote at my head, a glass of wine in my face [...] She has a need for conflict, a need for violence. It comes out of nowhere. The only thing I learned to do then was the same thing I used to do as a child (when his mother hit him, ed. note): retreat."

- Johnny Depp, during his interrogation on April 20, 2022.

Adam Waldman's statements

In April 2020, Depp's lawyer Adam Waldman stated in a *Daily* Mail article several allegations against Heard, three of which were upheld at the 2022 trial.

The first statement asserted that "Amber Heard and her friends in the media have used false allegations of sexual violence as both a sword and a shield, according to their needs. And thus selected some of these absurd facts of sexual violence as a sword, inflicting them on the public and on Mr. Depp"; the second - about a 2016 incident in the couple's Hollywood penthouse - that "it was simply an ambush, a hoax. They tricked Mr. Depp into calling the cops, but the first attempt didn't work. The officers came to the penthouse, carefully searched and questioned, and left after seeing no damage to the face or property. So Amber and her friends spilled some wine and trashed the room, prepared their stories under the guidance of a lawyer and a reporter, then made a second 911 call"; finally, the third statement assured, "We have reached the beginning of the end of Mme Heard's abusive hoax against Johnny Depp".

At the trial verdict on June 1er 2022, the jury concluded that the lawyer's second statement "was false, defamatory and committed with actual malice", which will cost Johnny Depp $2 million in compensation to Amber Heard.

Allegations against Johnny Depp

"I never want to lay eyes on that filthy whore Amber again [...] I'm going to fuck her burnt corpse afterwards, to make sure she's dead."""

- Excerpts from text messages Johnny Depp sent to friends and family about the actress.

In Amber Heard's countersuit, her lawyers point out that Vanessa Paradis, the mother of Depp's two children who has spoken out on several occasions in his defense, was insulted during their separation. In an e-mail to Elton John, the actor called her a "French extortionist" and a "bitch" who wanted to "brainwash" his children.

The lawyers also present a video clip from 2016, already revealed to the public at the time, showing Depp in the marital kitchen, angry and inebriated, where he can be seen slamming cupboard doors and pouring himself a glass of wine as Heard asks him questions and films him without his knowledge' . In another audio clip, the actor is heard yelling "shut up" at her as she accused him of "beating her up".

On May 5, Heard detailed the numerous acts of violence to which she was allegedly subjected by her ex-husband during a trip to Australia, claiming that these went as far as rape' . She had already made this claim at the trial in London, claiming that she had been held hostage for three days by the actor. She eventually had to retract her statement, admitting that she had a telephone at her disposal and multiple third parties coming in and out of the house. The London judge excused her, understanding that she had used "hyperbole".

"I have a hard time finding the words to describe how painful this is. It's horrible for me to sit here for weeks and relive everything [...].

He'd throw glasses, turn over tables, bang the walls very close to my face and shout at me. Then he'd disappear, wean himself off [...] Then he'd come back and give me so much love that I forgot how terrifying it was [...].

I'll never forget the first time he hit me [...] I didn't move because I didn't know what else to do [...] He hit me again. Hard. I lost my balance and realized the worst was about to happen [...] Then he started crying, I'd never seen a grown man cry. He cried his eyes out, got down on his knees and told me he wouldn't do it again. He said: "I thought I'd killed the monster, I won't do it again". I said nothing, went to my car and stayed there for a long time until I had the strength to know what I had to do. I was heartbroken."'

- Amber Heard on the first day of her hearing on Wednesday May 4.

Other legal problems

In 1989, Depp was arrested in his Vancouver hotel room for assaulting a security guard after the police had been called to break up a noisy party. He was arrested again in 1994 after ransacking a room at *The Mark Hotel* in New York, which he shared with Kate Moss'. The lawsuit against him was dropped after he agreed to pay damages. In 1999 in London, Depp was arrested again for fighting with paparazzi outside a restaurant while dining with Paradis'.

In 2012, UC Irvine medical professor Robin Eckert sued Depp and three security companies, claiming she was manhandled by his bodyguards at a Los Angeles concert in 2011. She was allegedly handcuffed and dragged 12 meters, resulting in injuries including a dislocated elbow. Depp's lawyers argued that Eckert had provoked this alleged assault and that she had therefore consented to "all battery". Eckert's court documents, on the other hand, state that Depp, despite being the direct manager of her security guards, did nothing to stop the assault. Before the case went to court, the actor is said to have settled with Eckert, offering him a certain sum of money.

In March 2016, Depp severed ties with his management company, *The Management Group* (TMG), and sued it in January 2017 for "mismanaging his money" and leaving him "more than $40 million in debt" . The company claims Depp was responsible for his own fiscal mismanagement and counter-sued him for unpaid fees. In a related case, Depp also sued his lawyer, Bloom Hergott, in January 2017. The two lawsuits are settled in 2018 and 2019 respectively.

In 2018, two of his former bodyguards sued him for unpaid fees and very poor working conditions; the case was settled in 2019 . Also in 2018, Depp was the subject of a complaint brought by stage manager Greg Brooks during the filming of *City of Lies* (2018), the latter accusing him of punching him twice while under the influence of alcohol, a claim denied by his lawyers and certain witnesses. Before the case reached court, a settlement was reached between Depp and the technical crew member in July 2022.

Finally, the actor announced at a trial audition that he would never reprise his role as Jack Sparrow, due to his differences with Disney (as was the case in 2020 with Warner in his role as Gellert Grindelwald). During the filming of the fifth *Pirates of the Caribbean movie,* Depp was reportedly constantly "drunk, alcoholic and unmanageable", according to members of the technical crew. "He disrupted the smooth running of the shoot with his completely erratic behavior. He often seemed to be late, forcing the crew to wait for hours.

Verdict

After six weeks of trial, the last day of closing arguments took place on May 27, giving Heard and Depp's legal teams one last chance to convince the seven jurors"""". The latter then retired for deliberations, with Judge Penney Azcarate asking them to confirm or not the *actual* malicious defamation that Amber Heard allegedly inflicted on Johnny Depp by writing this *Washington Post* op-ed. For her to be judged for actual malice (also known as *compensatory damage, the* US legal standard for defamation cases, determining whether agents or celebrities can recover damages in lawsuits) and therefore lose the case, she must have written her op-ed "knowing her allegations were false, or with reckless disregard for whether they were false or not".

The verdict came down on June 1er after five days of deliberation. The jurors found Amber Heard guilty of "defamation with actual malice" against Johnny Depp for her statements in the Washington Post op-ed. They ordered her to pay $10 million in *compensatory damages* and $5 million in *punitive* damages, reduced to $350,000 in accordance with Virginia state law, which caps punitive damages at this amount" . The actress must therefore pay a total of **$10.35 million** to her ex-husband"" .

In Heard's countersuit against Depp's lawyer, Adam Waldman, the jury found that Waldman's first and third statements about "false allegations of sexual violence" and "false abuse" were truthful and non-defamatory" . However, it concluded that Waldman's second statement to the *Daily Mail* - stating that "Heard and his friends wanted to frame Mr. Depp by calling the cops" - was false, defamatory and committed "with actual malice". As a result, Depp was ordered to pay **$2 million in** compensatory *damages*, but $0 in *punitive* damages" .

Reactions

Minutes after the verdict, both defendants immediately reacted on their social networks. Heard declared that the disappointment she felt was "beyond words": "I'm sad to have lost this case. But I'm even sadder to have lost a right I thought I had as an American: to speak freely and openly". Johnny Depp, for his part, welcomed the outcome: "False, very serious and criminal accusations were made against me through the media [...] These accusations went around the world twice in a nanosecond, with catastrophic consequences for my life and career. And 6 years later, the jury has given me my life back. I am deeply moved [...] From the outset, the aim of this case was to reveal the truth, whatever the outcome. Telling the truth was something I owed to my children and to all those who remained steadfast in their support for me. I feel at peace now, knowing that I have finally accomplished that".

According to legal experts at *Law&Crime,* two testimonies from Depp's camp would have changed the course of the trial . Firstly, that of British model Kate Moss, Depp's ex-wife, rejecting Heard's allegations that she had already been assaulted by the actor "even once" during their relationship between 1994 and 1998 . And secondly, that of metadata expert - Norbert Bryan Neumeister: when Amber Heard's team had shown several photographic evidence of bruises on her face and body that she claimed were caused by her ex-husband, Depp's lawyers had claimed that the actress had altered photos to make her injuries appear more severe. This was confirmed by the expert who stated that some of the files "did not match forensically" and that they "all had to undergo some type of transformation to change size", adding that thanks to the analysis of the Exif data, it could be seen that the photos did not come from a phone, but from an editing program" . Falsifications of the truth for which she could be imprisoned, according to Aaron Minc, a legal expert interviewed by *Geo News:* "She fabricated evidence, fabricated photos, fabricated bruises [...] I hope the prosecutors will take a close look at this. If there is very clear evidence that she tampered with evidence, that should be taken into account and could potentially lead to criminal prosecution and jail time" .

Calls and final agreement

A month later, in July 2022, Heard's lawyers appealed against the verdict, claiming a mistrial and that Depp's celebrity status, the presence of cameras in the courtroom and, above all, social networks had played an unhealthy role. "They demonized Amber Heard [...] Evidence was also suppressed between the trial in the UK and the one in the USA", says Elaine Bredehoft . This claim was rejected by the Judge, however, stating that there was "no evidence of fraud or wrongdoing" and that the composition of the jury had been approved by both parties . The actor's lawyers, who were ordered to pay Amber Heard $2 million, had also filed their own appeal.

On December 19, Amber Heard announced in a statement on Instagram that she had decided to settle the legal battle, declaring that even if her appeal were to succeed, she would "simply not be able to endure" a retrial, citing a financial and psychological toll: "I am making this decision after losing faith in the American legal system, where my unprotected testimony has served as entertainment and content for social networks." She asserts, however, that the agreement was "not an act of concession". "It's important for me to say that I never chose this," she wrote™ .

In a separate statement, Depp's lawyers Benjamin Chew and Camille Vasquez say that Heard has agreed to pay $1 million to end the case - far less than the jury verdict required her to pay. They claim, however, that the agreement was not a victory for the actress, writing that "the jury's unanimous decision and resulting judgment against Ms. Heard remain in full force and effect." "The payment of one million dollars - which Mr. Depp undertakes to donate to charity, which he will in fact do - demonstrates that Ms. Heard recognizes the conclusions of justice," they added. With this agreement, the actor's conviction by the courthouse has also been dropped" .

Media impact and the power of social networks

The Fairfax trial is becoming one of the most closely followed in the world. Whereas in London, the public was kept informed through court reports, the 2022 trial was filmed (which the plaintiffs welcomed) - as authorized by the judicial system - by *Court TV*, a US digital network specializing in criminal and legal analysis, and broadcast live on television, the Internet (Pluto TV, Twitch...) and, *ultimately,* social networks (Tiktok, YouTube, Twitter, Instagram...), where users freely expressed their opinions on the case'.

Various excerpts from the trial were the subject of video-compilations, video-reactions by users and memes, some of which went viral, reaching tens of millions of views" - and testifying to the intrinsic violence of the networks - for example, making a mockery of the actress's testimony on the stand, recounting an alleged rape, by Johnny Depp's supporters.

- LCI notes the hostility of a large proportion of Internet users towards Amber Heard, growing since several elements of her testimony were disputed: "Some have gone so far as to deconstruct her every word, claiming that she stole them from the film *The Talented Mr Ripley*. They think she acts when she cries, but doesn't do enough when she doesn't.".

- A petition on Change.org calling for the actress to be excluded from the film *Aquaman 2* reached over 4.6 million signatures in November 2022'. Making it one of the most signed petitions targeting an individual in the world.

- Excluding Elizabeth II, Johnny Depp was the most Googled personality in 2022, followed by Will Smith and Amber Heard'.

Impact on victims of domestic violence

- For Michele Dauber, professor of law at Stanford University, campaigner against sexual assault and defender of Amber Heard, this is "the worst court decision in decades for victims" and shows "a profound lack of understanding of sexual violence on the part of the Judge". According to her, Amber Heard had to "describe her alleged rape in graphic detail on television. This is shocking and should offend all women and victims, whether they agree with the verdict or not [...] The last time a rape victim was forced to testify publicly was in 1983". "There is no public interest in this case that could possibly outweigh the harm caused [...] [From now on] every victim will think twice before coming forward and applying for a restraining order or telling anyone about the abuse they have suffered." "Women can be hurt, even killed, because they don't call for help. This case has been a complete disaster. It is potentially catastrophic" concludes Dauber".

- "The trial has fascinated a global audience unaccustomed to looking at allegations of sexual assault within a couple, and that - regardless of opinions on the verdict - is a problem," Ruth Glenn, president of the *National Coalition Against Domestic Violence* (NCADV), also explains to AFP. "I don't think our society understands the dynamics of domestic violence yet [...] This crucial context has not been sufficiently discussed in the courtroom debates." She also asserts that there is "no doubt" about the types of abuse that were revealed at the trial. "We have to make sure that the people present understand that. But until we do that, don't show this kind of thing on TV" she warns'" .

- "The message is received. Tonight #MeToo is not dead. #MeToo has been killed," said Osez le féminisme! in response.

- Johnny Depp's camp denies allegations that Amber Heard's conviction is a punishment for victims of domestic violence. They point out that the jurors and Judge Penney Azcarate are experts, chosen specifically for their experience given that the defendants are both celebrities, and that the actor too had to describe in detail the "proven assaults" he suffered, providing photos, evidence and recordings, but also that several celebrities and feminist associations defended the actor'' .

Political views

In November 2016, Depp joined the *Imprisoned for Art* campaign to call for the release of Ukrainian filmmaker Oleg Sentsov, who was being held in Russia.

During the 2016 US presidential election campaign, he supported Democratic candidate Hillary Clinton and would later criticize President Donald Trump several times″ .

Filmography

1980s

- 1984: *A Nightmare on Elm Street* by Wes Craven: Glen Lantz
- 1985: *Private Resort* by George Bowers: Jack Marshall
- 1986: *Platoon* by Oliver Stone: Lerner

1990s

- 1990: *Cry-Baby* by John Waters: Wade "Cry-Baby" Walker
- 1990: *Edward Scissorhands* by Tim Burton: Edward
- 1991: *Freddy's Dead: The Final Nightmare* by Rachel Talalay: Glen Lantz / Oprah Noodlemantra, cameo
- 1992 : *Arizona Dream* by Emir Kusturica : Axel Blackmar
- 1993: *Benny and Joon* by Jeremiah S. Chechik: Sam
- 1993: *Gilbert Grape* by Lasse Hallström: Gilbert Grape
- 1994: *Ed Wood* by Tim Burton: Edward D. Wood Jr.

- 1994: *Don Juan DeMarco* by Jeremy Leven: Don Juan/John R. DeMarco
- 1995: *Dead Man* by Jim Jarmusch: William Blake
- 1995: *Murder in Suspense* (*Nick of Time*) by John Badham: Gene Watson
- 1996: *Cannes Man* by Richard Martini: himself
- 1997: *Donnie Brasco* by Mike Newell: Donnie Brasco / Joseph D. Pistone
- 1997: *The Brave* by himself (director and screenwriter): Raphael
- 1998: *Las Vegas Parano* by Terry Gilliam: Raoul Duke
- 1998: *I Love L.A.* by Mika Kaurismäki: himself (cameo)
- 1999: Roman Polanski's *The Ninth Gate*: Dean Corso
- 1999: *Intrusion* by Rand Ravich: Spencer Armacost
- 1999: *Sleepy Hollow: Legend of the Headless Horseman* (*Sleepy Hollow*) by Tim Burton: Ichabod Crane

2000s

- 2000: *Les Larmes d'un homme* (*The Man Who Cried*) by Sally Potter: César
- 2000: Julian Schnabel's *Avant la nuit* (*Before Night Falls*): Lt. Victor, "Bon Bon".
- 2000: *Le Chocolat* (*Chocolat*) by Lasse Hallström: Roux

- 2001: *Blow* by Ted Demme: George Jung
- 2001: *From Hell* by Albert and Allen Hughes: Inspector Frederich Abberline
- 2002: *Lost in La Mancha* by Keith Fulton and Louis Pepe (documentary): himself
- 2003: *Pirates of the Caribbean*: The *Curse of the Black Pearl* by Gore Verbinski: Captain Jack Sparrow
- 2003: Once Upon a *Time in Mexico... Desperado 2* (*Once Upon a Time in Mexico*) by Robert Rodriguez: Sheldon Sands
- 2004: *Secret Window* by David Koepp: Morton Rainey
- 2004: *Ils se marièrent et eurent beaucoup d'enfants* by Yvan Attal: L'inconnu (cameo)
- 2004: *Neverland* by Marc Forster: Sir James Matthew Barrie
- 2004: *Rochester, the Last of the Libertines* (*The Libertine*) by Laurence Dunmore: John Wilmot, 2e Earl of Rochester
- 2005: *Charlie and the Chocolate Factory* by Tim Burton: Willy Wonka
- 2005: *Corpse Bride* by Tim Burton: Victor Van Dort (voice)
- 2006: *Pirates of the Caribbean: Dead Man's Chest* by Gore Verbinski: Captain Jack Sparrow

- 2007: *Pirates of the Caribbean: At World's End* by Gore Verbinski: Captain Jack Sparrow
- 2007: *Sweeney Todd: The Demon Barber of Fleet Street* by Tim Burton: Sweeney Todd / Benjamin Barker
- 2009: Terry Gilliam's *The Imaginarium of Doctor Parnassus*: Tony (1re transformation)
- 2009: Michael Mann's *Public Enemies*: John Dillinger

Year 2010

- 2010: *When You're Strange* by Tom DiCillo (documentary on The Doors): narrator
- 2010: *Alice* in *Wonderland* by Tim Burton: The Mad Hatter
- 2010: *The Tourist* by Florian Henckel von Donnersmarck: Frank Tupelo
- 2011: *Rango* by Gore Verbinski: Rango (voice)
- 2011: *Pirates of the Caribbean: On Stranger Tides* by Rob Marshall: Captain Jack Sparrow
- 2011: *Rhum express* (*The Rum Diary*) by Bruce Robinson: Paul Kemp
- 2011: *Jack and Julie* (*Jack and Jill*) by Dennis Dugan: himself
- 2012: *21 Jump Street* by Phil Lord and Chris Miller: Officer Tom Hanson
- 2012: *Dark Shadows* by Tim Burton: Barnabas Collins

- 2013 : *Lone Ranger: Birth of a Hero* (*The Lone Ranger*) by Gore Verbinski: Tonto
- 2013 : *Lucky Them* by Megan Griffiths: Matthew Smith (cameo)
- 2014: *Transcendence* (*Transcendence*) by Wally Pfister: Will
- 2014: *Tusk* by Kevin Smith: Guy LaPointe
- 2015: *Into the Woods* by Rob Marshall: the wolf
- 2015: *Charlie Mortdecai* (*Mortdecai*) by David Koepp: Charlie Mortdecai
- 2015: *Strictly Criminal* (*Black Mass*) by Scott Cooper: Whitey Bulger
- 2016 : *Alice Through the Looking Glass* by James Bobin: the Mad Hatter
- 2016: *Yoga Hosers* by Kevin Smith: Guy LaPointe
- 2016 : *Fantastic Beasts and Where to Find Them* by David Yates: Gellert Grindelwald
- 2017: *Pirates of the Caribbean: Salazar's Revenge* (*Pirates of the Caribbean: Dead Men Tell No Tales*) by Joachim Rønning and Espen Sandberg: Captain Jack Sparrow
- 2017 : Kenneth Branagh's Murder *on the Orient Express*: Samuel Ratchett / John Cassetti
- 2018 : *Fatal seduction* (*London Fields*) by Matthew Cullen : Chick Purchase (cameo)
- 2018: *City of Lies* by Brad Furman: Russell Poole

- 2018 : *Fantastic Beasts: The Crimes of Grindelwald* by David Yates: Gellert Grindelwald
- 2018 : *Brothers in Arms* by Paul Sanchez: himself
- 2018: *Sherlock Gnomes*: Sherlock Gnomes (voice)
- 2019 : *The Last Days of Mr. Brown* (*The Professor*) by Wayne Roberts: Richard

2020s

- 2020: *Waiting for the Barbarians* by Ciro Guerra : Colonel Joll
- 2020: *Minamata* by Andrew Levitas: William Eugene Smith
- 2023: Maïwenn's *Jeanne du Barry*: Louis XV
- 2024: Johnny Depp's *Modi*

Video game

- 2006: *Pirates of the Caribbean: The Legend of Jack Sparrow*: Jack Sparrow'

1980s

- 1985: *Lady Blue* by John Florea and John D. Hancock (season 1, episode 4): Lionel Viland
- 1986: *Death in Troubled Waters* by Matthew Chapman (TV movie): Donnie Fleischer
- 1987: Aaron Spelling's *Hotel* (season 4, episode 15): Rob Cameron
- 1987-1990: *21 Jump Street* by Stephen J. Cannell and Patrick Hasburgh (71 episodes): Officer Tom Hanson

2000s

- 2004: *King of the Hill* by Mike Judge and Greg Daniels (season 8, episode 20): Yogi Victor (voice)
- 2009: *SpongeBob SquarePants* by Stephen Hillenburg (season 6, episode 21): Jack Kahuna Laguna, "The Surf King" (voice)

Year 2010

- 2011: Life's Too Short by Ricky Gervais and Stephen Merchant (season 1, episode 2): himself
- 2012: Joe Vaux's *The Griffins* (*Family Guy*) (season 11, episode 6): Edward Scissorhands (voice)
- 2016: *The Walking Dead* (season 6, episode 12): severed head (cameo)

Cinema

- He appears under the pseudonym *Oprah Noodlemantra* in a TV commercial in the film *The End of Freddy: The Ultimate Nightmare* (1991).
- In 1998, he appeared in his own role and as *William Blake* in Mika Kaurismäki's *I Love L.A.*.
- In 2004, he appeared in Yvan Attal's film *Ils se marièrent et eurent beaucoup d'enfants.*

Television

- He played himself in 1999 in an episode of the British TV series *The Vicar of Dibley* and in 2000 in a sketch for the entertainment show *The Fast Show*.

- He lends his face in the television series The Walking Dead in the episode *Not Tomorrow Yet (*Season 6, Episode 12), as the head model of a *prowler.*

Animation series

- He lends his voice to the character of *Yogi Victor* in the original version of *King of the Hill*, and plays himself in the third season of *American Dad!* (episode *Tearjerker* - 2008). He also lends his voice to *Jack Kahuna Laguna*, *The Surf King* in an episode of *SpongeBob SquarePants* (*The Perfect Wave* - 2009).

Documentaries

- In 1996, for the TV mini-series *American States of Poetry*, Johnny Depp read *chorus 113* from *Mexico City Blues* by beatnik writer Jack Kerouac. Three years later, he took part in Chuck Workman's Beat Generation documentary *The Source*, where he again read from a text by Jack Kerouac.
- In 2008, he was the narrator of Gonzo: The Life and Work of D. Thompson, a documentary tribute to his friend and writer Hunter S. Thompson.

Thompson, *Gonzo: The Life and Work of D^r. Hunter S. Thompson*.

- He was also the voiceover for Tom DiCillo's 2010 documentary film about The Doors, *When You're Strange.*

Audio books

- He is a reader of Keith Richards' autobiography *Life*, published in audio form in 2011.

Advertising and the arts

H&M in 1999

In 2015, Johnny Depp became the face of *Dior Sauvage* fragrance' . Despite Hollywood's boycott of his accusations of domestic violence, the haute couture house supported him and signed a new contract with him in November 2021. The actor became the face of the brand's latest fragrance: *Sauvage Elixir* .

In collaboration with the Duesenberg brand, he designed a signature guitar model with all his tattoos drawn on it, as well as a design and pickup made just for him.

A text by Johnny Depp, translated by Virginie Despentes, appeared in 2008 in an issue of *Bordel magazine* devoted to Jean-Michel Basquiat' .

The actor promoted the work of French painter Thierry Alonso Gravleur by dedicating an exhibition to him at the Trigg Ison Gallery in Los Angeles in 2006 and 2011.

Music

Since 2015, Johnny Depp has been a member of the band Hollywood Vampires alongside Alice Cooper and Joe Perry (Aerosmith guitarist). They are the authors of a homonymous album released on September 11, 2015.

In July 2022, he records album *18* with Jeff Beck. The album features a majority of covers and a few original songs.

Recordings

- In 1994, Johnny Depp played guitar on the track *That Woman's Got Me Drinking from* Shane MacGowan's album *The Snake* ;
- In 1995, he recorded the album *P* with Gibby Haynes, Steve Jones, Flea, Chuck E. Weiss and Sal Jenco;
- he plays slide guitar on the Oasis song *Fade In-Out on the* 1997 album *Be Here Now.* He was invited by the band to play again the following year on *Fade Away* ;
- In 2000, he composed the music for two songs on his partner Vanessa Paradis's album *Bliss*: *St Germain* and *Bliss* ;
- He also played three guitar tracks in Lasse Hallström's 2001 film *Le Chocolat*, and contributed to the soundtrack of the film *Il était une fois au Mexique... Desperado 2* in 2003, composing a track (*Sands Theme*) credited under the pseudonym *Tonto's Giant Nuts* ;
- Vanessa Paradis took part in a tribute album to Alain Bashung, released in April 2011, in which

she covered the song *Angora*, produced, arranged and guitar-played by Johnny Depp ;

- In November 2011, the couple recorded a duet of the song *Ballade de Melody Nelson*, by Serge Gainsbourg and Jane Birkin, on the album *To Gainsbourg from Lulu,* produced by Lulu Gainsbourg ;
- In 2012, he played guitar on the cover of Carly Simon's *You're So Vain*, a bonus track on Marilyn Manson's 8ᵉ album, *Born Villain*. That same year, he took part in the *Banga* album by his friend Patti Smith;
- In 2013, he composed the music for the track *New Year* on Vanessa Paradis' album *Love Songs*.

Scene

- In November 1999, Johnny Depp took part in the private concert *Night Clubbing* organized by the French television channel Canal+, in which he accompanied Iggy Pop, Vanessa Paradis and Chrissie Hynde on guitar on several songs;
- he joined Vanessa Paradis on stage at the Olympia on March 25, 2001, for the last of the singer's concerts, accompanying her on guitar on a cover of Jacques Dutronc : *Fais pas ci, fais pas ça* ;

- he accompanied Eddie Vedder and Patti Smith at the *Voices For Justice* concert in Little Rock on August 28, 2010 ;
- a fan of hard rock singer Alice Cooper, he joined Cooper on guitar for two tracks at a concert on June 28, 2011 ;
- On April 11, 2012, he accompanied his friend Marilyn Manson on guitar in concert in Los Angeles, on two songs: *Sweet Dreams* and *The Beautiful People* ;
- In June 2018 and 2023, he takes part in Hellfest (Clisson) with his band Hollywood Vampires.

Clips

- Johnny Depp appeared in Tom Petty's 1991 video *Into The Great Wide Open* ;
- In 1994, he starred in the video clip for Shane MacGowan's song *That Woman's Got Me Drinking* ;
- In 2006, he was featured in the posthumous Johnny Cash video *God's Gonna Cut You Down*, along with some thirty other artists;
- In 2008 and 2010, he appeared in the clips *L'Incendie* and *Il y a,* directed by his partner Vanessa Paradis;
- In 2012, he starred alongside Natalie Portman in Paul McCartney's *My Valentine* video, a song from the album *Kisses on the Bottom* released the

same year. In this clip, the two actors interpret the song's text in American Sign Language (ASL);

- In 2013, he starred alongside a host of artists in Paul McCartney's *Queenie Eye* video, a song from the album *New* released the same year;
- In 2014, he starred alongside bluesmen Roy Gaines and Al Williams, among others, in Paul McCartney's *Early Days* video, a song from the album *New* ;
- In 2017, he appeared in the Say10 and KILL4ME clips from the Heaven Upside Down album, in which he faced his interpreter, Marilyn Manson.

Awards

This section summarizes the main awards and nominations won by Johnny Depp. For a more complete list, please refer to the Internet Movie Database.

- For *Pirates of the Caribbean: The Curse of the Black Pearl*, he was nominated for 19 awards and won 4.
- For *Neverland,* he was nominated for 13 awards and won 1.
- For *Charlie and the Chocolate Factory*, he was nominated for 8 awards and won 4.
- For *Pirates of the Caribbean: The Secret of the Cursed Chest*, he was nominated for 11 awards and won 7.

- For *Pirates of the Caribbean: At World's End*, he was nominated for 4 awards and won 3.
- For *Sweeney Todd: The Evil Barber of Fleet Street*, he was nominated for 9 awards and won 5.

Other books by United Library

https://campsite.bio/unitedlibrary

Printed in the USA
CPSIA information can be obtained
at www.ICGtesting.com
LVHW012251050124
768170LV00016B/1204

9 789464 900507